25 minutes to enhance your Attitude Management

compiled by : Subhash C. Sethi

25 Minutes to Enhance Your

Attitude Management

Compiled by :
Subhash C. Sethi

First Published : 2003

ISBN 81-242-0329-6

Published by :

INDIANA BOOKS

For Crest Publishing House

G-2, 16 Ansari Road,

Darya Ganj, New Delhi - 110 002

326 0651, 326 0618

e-mail : sethidel@del6.vsnl.net.in

Printed at :

Saurabh Print-O-Pack

A-16, Sector-IV, Noida

Introduction

It is said, "Behaviour is a mirror in which everyone displays his image." However, behaviour itself is modelled by one's attitude.

The attitude of people, negative or positive, constructive or destructive, has its effects on every walk of human life. This is especially true of the management world which has teamwork as its focus. Attitude can make or mar the progress and development of any organisation.

An organisation will be exceptionally lucky if it possesses in its workforce only people with "just the right attitude". Such an organisation exists only in dreams, not in reality. A handful of difficult people make their way into big and small organisations. Their attitudes pose problems not only in getting work done from them, but infects the whole organisation. You may hate these employees, but cannot simply chuck them off for they are indispensable to your organisation. Managing the attitude of this handful, therefore, becomes challenging for any and every manager.

Not only these troublesome few, but others as well, who are otherwise fine people, need to undergo attitudinal training to become more useful and productive to the company.

"25 Minutes To Enhance Your Attitude Management" provides wonderful suggestions to handle your employees. The tips given in the book are useful, and not only for managing employees. Readers in general can also treat these as auto suggestions to improve their overall personality and join the list of achievers.

25 minutes

Remember that most irritating people believe their behaviour is reasonable and acceptable.

25 minutes

Watch out for prima donnas. Among the most irritating of people, they have become legends in their own minds.

You can be social minded without being a socialist.

History abounds with tales of experts who were convinced that the ideas, plans and projects of others could never be achieved. However, accomplishment came to those who said, "I can make it happen."

Forget about 'attitude'. Instead, focus on behaviour. It's the only thing an executive can identify and – hopefully – change.

The secret principle of human nature is the craving to be appreciated.

Each of us has the responsibility to put our world together. It starts by getting ourselves put together. We can become better parents, friends, partners, employees and employers. The first step is changing our attitude.

Make sure of your value to the organisation – or of your marketability – before taking on an irritating boss.

There is always an easy solution to every human problem – neat, plausible and wrong.

Behaviourism is a kind of flat-earth view of the mind.

25 minutes

Analyze and categorise an artist first. This helps you develop a clearer strategy for managing them.

How one perceives or interprets someone's attitude depends on his background, experience, priorities and prejudices.

Wisdom is not a product of schooling, but of the lifelong attempt to acquire it.

Don't be deceived by cheerleaders. Their incessant attempts to flatter are meant to keep your attention away from their poor productivity.

One of the first steps to accomplish great things in your life is to cease dwelling on the negative things in your past. Carefully assess your present strengths, successes and achievements.

Dwell on the positive events in your life and quit limiting your potential by constantly thinking about what you have done poorly.

25 minutes…

Be careful when confiding your inmost thoughts to co-workers, especially to subordinates. Your words may come back to bite you.

Man is still the most inexpensive, non linear, all-purpose computing system that is capable of being mass-produced by unskilled labour.

Everything we experience and everybody we encounter will carry the scent we hold in our mind.

Don't let procrastinators jeopardise deadlines and force snap decisions.

Personal relations are the important things for ever and ever, and not the outer life of telegrams and anger.

Every great achievement was once impossible until someone set a goal to make it a reality.

An executive should keep the know-it-all off balance by refusing to play the role of a student. He will only encourage more condescending behaviour.

Nothing shakes the morale of an organisation as much as the sudden lowering of the boom on an individual without prior notice to improve his deficiencies.

God and the devil are an effort towards specialisation and division of labour.

Do your best to open up clams. They often harbour some tasty morsels of insight and innovation.

An unfulfilled vocation drains the colour from a man's entire existence.

If one thinks one is beaten, one is. If one thinks one dare not, one does not! If one wants to win, but thinks one can't, it's almost a cinch one won't.

25 minutes…

Don't allow wafflers to delay a decision until time becomes critical.

Contrary to the belief that workers are not interested in their company, most employees want more information relating to their role in the company.

It is important that employees identify with the company, that they are made to feel part of it and not just a number.

Keep a lid on jolly jokers. They can derail team efforts and morale awfully fast.

There is little friendship in the world, and least of all between equals.

It is essential to state policies of recognition for jobs well done, rewards for ideas, a policy of promotion from within and news publicity for accomplishments.

Don't debate with jolly jokers about the value of their humour. They'll say you can't take a joke. Instead, show how their behaviour is disrupting work.

A sense of duty is useful in work, but offensive in personal relations. People wish to be liked, not be endured with patient resignation.

To find out what staff members think, meet them. These sessions should deal specifically with performance and be an opportunity to exchange thoughts, insights and suggestions for improvement.

Watch worrywarts closely. Left unmanaged, they can cause mass panic among your work group.

Every manufacturer ought to remember that his fortune was not achieved by himself alone, but by the cooperation of his workmen. He should acknowledge their rights to share the benefits of that which could not exist without their faithful performance of duty.

Human relations can be described as the integration of people into groups that can work together harmoniously and positively for the economic benefit and social satisfaction of all.

Turn a naysayer into a 'Yea' sayer by taking a negative position. They'll counter it by taking a positive approach.

Super achievers think in ways that make them less sensitive to disapproval and rejection. They brush off rejection faster.

The rules of fair play require that a person be told where he stands and why.

Avoid genetic jerks. They have an inborn tendency to be aggravating.

In the field of modern business, so rich in opportunity for the exercise of man's finest and most varied mental faculties and moral qualities, mere money-making cannot be regarded as the legitimate end...since with the conduct of business, human happiness or misery is inextricably interwoven.

The fact is that the possession of a highly sensitive social conscience about large-scale issues is no guarantee whatsoever of reasonable conduct in private relations.

Handle psychotics with care. They may be out of touch with reality.

Subconscious thoughts, when expressed, become your attitude.

Most men are like eggs, too full of themselves to hold anything else.

Tap into the experience that cynical old-timers have. Just do your best to hold their cynicism at bay.

Expect to encounter irritating people in the workplace. That way, the experience won't be as much of a shock.

To find out what sort of person 'they' are, one must go to 'them'.

Don't let information misers clog up your organisation. It thrives on timely information that must flow freely.

Some folks are wise,
and some are otherwise.

If you are the boss, just remember that your attitude is always showing.

Watch your back. Saboteurs prefer stealth and sneak attacks.

*People have one thing in common:
They are all different.*

*It seems a pity that psychology should
have destroyed all knowledge of
human nature.*

25 minutes...

When dealing with fast-talking lousy listeners, slow the pace of your speech. They'll usually slow down, too.

There are two kinds of people: those who don't do what they want to do, so they write down in a diary what they haven't done, and those who have no time to write about it, because they're out doing it.

The trouble with business is people. A machine will never go off in a corner and sulk – but people will. A machine will never make a mistake, but people will. A machine will never show off, leave early or argue with the boss, but people will.

Under no circumstance should you show time bombs special deference. It only encourages them and undermines your authority.

There are people who are too stupid to have prejudices.

Some people seem as if they can never have been children, and others seem as if they could never be anything else.

With time bombs, stay cool and be sure not to act intimidated. They love to throw people off balance with their outbursts.

Almost every person, if you believe him, holds quite a different theory of life from the one on which he is presently acting.

People don't change, they only become more so.

Dig in and stand your ground with steamrollers. They need to understand that they don't have a lock on all the good ideas.

Men have a trick of coming up to what is expected of them, good or bad.

It is only when we are misunderstood by others that we really understand ourselves.

Manage whiners carefully. Like worrywarts, they can spread their aggravating behaviour to other members of the work group.

Encourage employees to praise each other.

Remove personality conflicts between your employees and if they still persist, fire the incurable person so that he can work for your competitors.

Call a whiner's bluff by confronting the person directly: "What is the problem? What can I do to help the situation?"

In the study of Man, it is easier to understand the species than the individual.

Monkeys are superior to men in this: When a monkey looks into a mirror, he sees a monkey.

Don't ask people at work to assess your personality critically. The request may be misinterpreted by the person you ask.

Keep strong, if possible. In any case, keep cool. Have unlimited patience. Never corner an opponent and always assist him to save his face. Put yourself in his shoes and see things through his eyes. Avoid self-righteousness like the devil. Nothing is so self-blinding.

A real superior man is like a bell. If you ring it, it rings, and if you don't, it does not, as the saying goes.

Heed your performance evaluations. They can be excellent sources of feedback about your irritating behaviour.

Most people are hidden most of the time, their appearances are brief and controlled, their movements secret, the outlines of their lives obscured.

One really understands in others only those feelings that he is capable of producing himself.

Take the grapevine's feedback with a grain of salt, but admit to yourself that it could be on target.

People are always sincere.
They change sincerities, that's all.

If you do not understand a man, you cannot crush him. And if you do understand him, very probably you will not.

If people are avoiding you, find out why.
The answer may save your career.

We would know mankind better if we were not so anxious to resemble one another.

People are made alarming by one's dread of their unremitting, purposeful continuity.

People are the corporation, not machinery and the plant. But there is one complication, some you can lead and some you can't.

Teach employees to accept criticism as part of their job and to learn from it. Take criticism for what it is worth and nothing more.

Kill anger. Anger is something that can create long term problems and that too big ones.

25 minutes

It's not the hundred-and-one problems of production and distribution that keep executives awake at night trying to solve them; it's the problems of working with people, the human problems of their jobs.

To observe a man, observe how he wins his object, rather than how he loses it; for when we fail, our pride supports us, when we succeed, it betrays us.

Encourage employees to encourage each other.

What makes men happy is loving to do what they have to. This is the principle on which society is founded.

A child-like man is not a man whose development has been arrested; on the contrary, he is a man who has given himself a chance of continuing to develop long after most adults have muffled themselves in the cocoon of middle-aged habits and conventions.

It is always safe to assume that people are more subtle and less sensitive than they seem.

If you improve workers' morale and strengthen their sense of belonging, you create a cooperative spirit that results in better work.

Emperors, kings, artisans, peasants, big people, little people, at the bottom people are all alike and all the same, all just alike on the inside, and when the clothes are off, nobody can tell who is who.

It is no wonder that people were so horrible when they started life as children.

25 minutes

Almost all relationships begin, and most of them continue, as forms of mutual exploitation, a mental or physical barter to be terminated when one or both parties run out of goods.

If you do to others what you would like them to do to you, do not expect others to do to you what you do to them.

There are people whom one would very well like to drop, but would not wish to be dropped by.

The employer puts his money and the workman his life. The one has as much right as the other to regulate the business.

Understand that people usually believe it's the other person who's being aggravating or unreasonable.

Be free of all prejudices. Treat everyone equally.

If the worker has a sense of belonging, he will be much more contented with his work.

People are too durable, that's their main trouble. They can do too much to themselves, they last too long.

You can't have everything in one person.

There's nothing so exhausting as the management of men, except the management of women.

If the attitude of the boss, the trainer or the trainee is not right, nothing else can be right.

It is so pleasant to come across people more stupid than ourselves. We love them at once for being so.

The voice of dissent must be heard.

Don't believe in the goodness of disagreeable people.

Working with people is difficult, but not impossible.

Believe in the supreme worth of the individual, and in his right to life, liberty and the pursuit of happiness.

It is less dangerous to treat most men badly than to treat them too well.

Nothing between human beings is one to three. In fact, all life is six to five.

Office and plant morale should be a continuous state. When a mere smile and a nod from the boss causes an unaccustomed ripple of happiness to flow over an office, that's a bad sign. It's a sign that up to that moment, people had been tense, harassed, fearful, nervous and worried.

Don't judge any man until you have walked two moons in his moccasins.

There are four sorts of men: they who know not and know not they know not: they are fools, shun them; they who know not and know they know not: they are simple, teach them; they who know and know not they know: they are asleep, wake them; they who know and know they know: they are wise, follow them.

Gratitude preserves old friendships and procures new.

No matter how much work a man can do,
no matter how engaging his personality,
he will not advance far in business
if he cannot work through others.

Substitute the word "behaviour" for "attitude". Behaviour is tangible and much easier to describe.

People only see what they are prepared to see.

Not all of those to whom we do good love us. Neither do all those to whom we do evil hate us.

If there is any magic word in the management of business, it is the word attitude.

The man who desires to improve human beings must begin by appreciating them.

Draw from others the lessons that may profit yourself.

A positive attitude has to be built up continuously.

You never know till you try to reach them how accessible men are, but you must approach each man from the right door.

The greatness of a man can nearly always be measured by his willingness to be kind.

Among giants, try and be a dwarf; among dwarfs, try and be a giant; but among equals, try and be an equal.

Make your people feel more important by taking a serious, personal interest in their work. Let them know that the measure of their success is also the measure of success of their company or department.

He who thinks he can find in himself the means of doing without others is much mistaken; but he who thinks that others cannot do without him is still more mistaken.

Judge a person by the way he treats somebody who can be of no use to him.

Titles in the
25 MINUTES TO ENHANCE Series

Hiring Ability
Training Tact
Customer Selling
Leadership
Cost Cutting
Organisation Skills
Finance Management
Work Delegation
Decisions
Discretion
Presentation
Goals
Attitude Management
Performance Review
Influence
Motivation
Quality Management
Performance